# Pusheen the Cat's
## Guide to Everything

# Also by Claire Belton

# Pusheen the Cat's
## Guide to Everything

**Claire Belton**

**G** Gallery Books

New York London Toronto Sydney New Delhi

Gallery Books
An Imprint of Simon & Schuster, Inc.
1230 Avenue of the Americas
New York, NY 10020

First Gallery Books trade paperback edition January 2023

For information about special discounts for bulk purchases, please contact Simon &
Schuster Special Sales at 1-866-506-1949 or business@simonandschuster.com.

The Simon & Schuster Speakers Bureau can bring authors to your live event. For more
information or to book an event, contact the Simon & Schuster Speakers Bureau at
1-866-248-3049 or visit our website at www.simonspeakers.com.

Interior design by Davina Mock-Maniscalco

Manufactured in China

3  5  7  9  10  8  6  4  2

Library of Congress Control Number: 2022944844

ISBN 978-1-9821-6541-3
ISBN 978-1-9821-6542-0 (ebook)

For Sarah and Jake

# Contents

# Pusheen the Cat's
## Guide to Everything

# Pusheen

**GENDER:** Girl

**BIRTHDAY:** February 18

**BEST FEATURE:** Big body, small feet

**FAVORITE FOOD:** All of them

**FAVORITE COLOR:** Cream

**HOBBIES:** Being online, snacking, sleeping

**ATTRIBUTES:** Sweet, curious, lazy

# Pusheen's Guide to Fitting In

Plop

Squish

Squash

Ploink

# Pusheen's Guide to Crafts

## See an idea

## Buy supplies

# Harder than you thought

# See ANOTHER idea

Pudeen

# Pusheen's Purrfect Pairings

## Cappuccino
### +
## Cinnamon roll

## Macchiato
### +
## Madeleines

## Mocha
## +
## Macarons

## Coffee
## +
## Donuts

# Which One Are You?

**Coffee**
Full of beans
Dependable

**Croisssant**
Many layers
A little flaky

**Iced mocha**
Pretty chill
Sweet

**Madeleines**
Delicate
Charming

**Latte**
Easygoing
Creative

**Cappuccino**
Sophisticated
Romantic

**Matcha latte**
Energetic
Fluffy

**Muffin**
Wholesome
Nourishing

# Activities to Do
# with Your Cat

## Reading

## Puzzles

Gaming

Paranormal investigating

# Cat Classes

Geography

Psychology

Physics

History

# Pusheen's Guide to Hiding Places

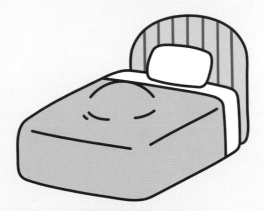

**Excellent**

**Great**

**Good**

**Terrible**

# How to Catch a Leprechaun

Put gold in a pot

Find a rainbow

Catch him!!

Share the wealth

# How to Make Your Own Luck

Find a 4-leaf clover

Spot a rainbow

Wish on a star

Get a horseshoe

# Irish Mytholosheens

## Leprechauneen

## Faireen

**Selkeen**

**Bansheen**

# Cat Sommelier

Unsophisticated, bland

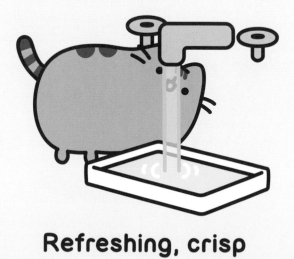

Refreshing, crisp

Notes of fish

Forbidden, sublime

# The ~~Dog~~ Cat Days of Summer

Too hot outside

Too hot inside

Too hot to sleep

~~Too hot to eat~~

# How to Befriend a Mermaid

## 1. Follow her siren call

## 2. Introduce yourself politely

## 3. Success

# How to Eat Ice Cream

On a cone

In a dish

Through a straw

From the source

# Pusheen's Guide to Staying Cool

## Keep hydrated

## Take a cool shower

## Find some shade(s)

## Be you

# Beach Day with Pusheen & Friends

wiches
Building sand~~castles~~

Frizzy
~~Frisbee~~ all day

Throwing
~~Finding~~ shade

Sand
~~Sunbathing~~

Bird
~~People~~ watching

~~Swimming~~

# What's Your Road Trip Job?

The navigator

The DJs

The snacker

The napper

The driver

# Signs You May Be a
# Cat Parent

## You teach them right from wrong

## You keep them entertained

You prepare all
of their meals

You love them
unconditionally

# Home Types for Cats

Condo

Duplex

Mobile home

Tree house

Castle

Dream home

# Fancy Outings
# (for Your Cat)

Expectation

Reality

Expectation

Reality

Expectation

Reality

# Which *Dessert* Are You?

### Ice cream sandwich
Always chilly
Sweet

### Éclair
Full of suprises
Fancy

### Swiss roll
Diplomat
Unique

### Mousse
Elegant
Smooth

**Donut**
Loves parties
Soft

**Dome cake**
Dressed to impress
Extra

**Cinnamon roll**
Early riser
Warm

**Tiramisu**
Always caffeinated
Multifaceted

# Yoga for Cats

Cat pose

Mountain pose

## Chair pose

## Happy baby pose

# Pusheen's TV Guide

**Weather forecast**

**Reality show**

## True crime

## Sci-fi

# Pusheenicorn's Guide to Horse Things

Horse blanket

Horse feed

Horse shoes

# Pusheen's Guide
# to Podcasting

## Get some gear

## Get your audio levels

## Get some guests

## Forget to hit record

# Pusheen's Guide to Baking Substitutions

Honey for sugar

Olive oil for butter

Vinegar for lemon juice Pans for other pans

Perfect!

# How to Make the Perfect Present

**Set a budget**

**Consider their interests**

**Go shopping**

**Get creative**

**Fill with cheer**

**Present!**

# Pusheen's Guide to Working from Home

## Get up on time

## Clear a work space

# Minimize distractions

# Utilize technology

# Pusheen's Guide to Constellations

**Big Pipper**

**Stormius**

**Sassyopeia**

# Cat Love Languages

## Words of affirmation

## Quality time

# Acts of service

# ~~Physical touch~~

# A Cat's Guide to the Arts

Painting

Sculpture

Music

Performance art

# Pusheen's Gourd Guide

Pumpsheen

Stormy pear

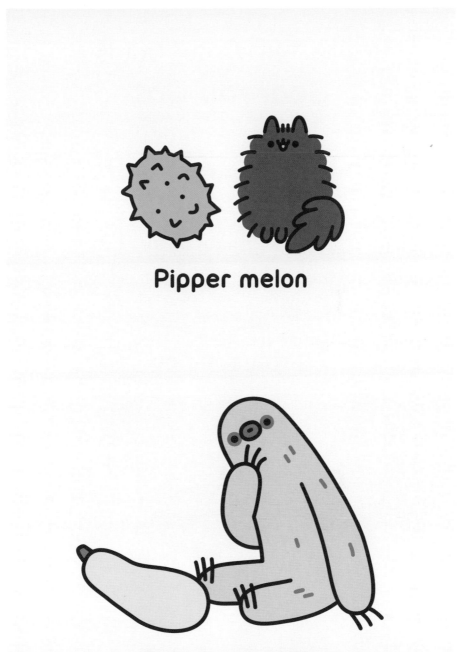

**Pipper melon**

**Butternut sloth**

# How to Tell If Your Cat Is a
# Scaredy Cat

## Always hiding

## Frequently jumpy

## Sees ghosts

## Good at screaming

# #GhostPerks
## with Boosheen the Ghost

Infinite snacks

Cold resistant

Maximum privacy

Always delighted

# How to Tell If Your Cat Is a
## *Vampurr*

### Sleeps in a box

### Has glowing eyes

Has fangs

Likes wet food

# Which One Are You?

### Kitten
Loves naps
Loves snacks

### Puppy
Enjoys walks
There for you

### Frog
Kinda jumpy
Questionable taste

### Alpaca
Big softie
Loves to frolic

## Flamingo
Tall
Excellent dancer

## Unicorn
Magical
Good at hiding

## Bunny
Good listener
Family oriented

## Owl
Wise
Never sleeps

# Desk Essentials for Cat People

Ergonomic chair

Wrist rest

## Hole puncher

## Desk toys

# Thanksgiving Roles

The "helper"

The decorator

The observer

The taste tester

# How to Define an Ideal Planet

## Has great resources

## Has a comfortable environment

## Has friendly locals

# Types of Snowmen

## Single scoop

## Double-decker

## Triple threat

## Decuple doom

# Winter Fashion
# (for Your Cat)

## Thick fleece

## A heavy coat

## Fuzzy mittens

## Layers

# What's Your *Holiday* Style?

Pusheen:
*The Classic*

Pastel Pusheen:
*The Futurist*

**Dragonsheen:**
*The Hoard*

**Mermaidsheen:**
*The Sunken Treasure*

**Super Pusheenicorn:**
*The Dreamscape*

**Dinosheen:**
*The Au Naturel*

# Pusheenicorn's Holiday Tips

**presence**
Gift your ~~presents~~

Be generous

## Light up the room

## Slay

# How to Plan for Christmas

## Wait for it . . .

## Wait for it . . .

# Celebrate!

# Wait for it . . .

# New Year's Day Checklist

☑ Get up

☑ Fill up

☑ Clean up

☑ Wrap up

# Pusheen's Winter Activities

## Sledding

## Skiing

**Skating**

**Snuggling**

# Sweater Weather

Smart

Sporty

Cozy

All natural

# Birthday Gift Ideas
# (for Your Cat)

## Something practical

## Something fun

## Something tasty

# Making History
# with Pusheenosaurus

**Survive**

**Thrive**

**Leave your mark**

I look up to remember

I stand in doorways to forget

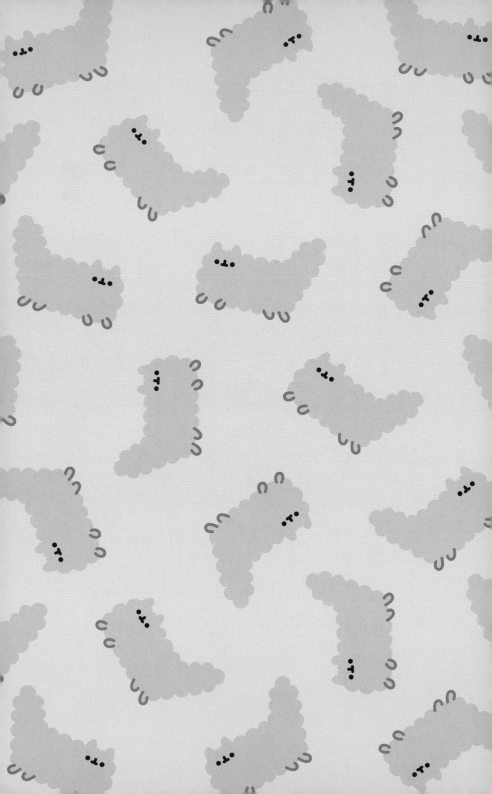

# Stormy

**GENDER:** Girl

**BIRTHDAY:** October 24

**BEST FEATURE:** Very curly

**FAVORITE FOOD:** Cookies & milk

**FAVORITE COLOR:** Pink

**HOBBIES:** Adventuring, grooming herself

**ATTRIBUTES:** Sweet, reliable, caring

# Types of Friends:
# The Angel

**Extremely pure**

**Very generous**

**Encourages good behavior**

When you spend so much
time with your sister you
start to dress like her

# Stormy's Guide
# to Getting Ready

**Scrub your scruff**

**Floof your fluff**

**Polish and buff**

**Strut your stuff**

# How to Annoy Your Big Sister

**Borrow her things**

**Get too nosy**

**Be too cute to get mad at**

# Uses for Extra Cat Hair

An itchy sweater

A strange wig

A creepy double

# Things Stormy Kinda Looks Like

Cotton candy

Sheep

Cloud

Shrub

# How to Identify a Middle Child

## Wears hand-me-downs

## Plays with hand-me-ups

Vies for attention

Surrounded with love

# Pusheen's Guide to Having a Little Sister

**Play together**

**Fight together**

## Scheme together

## Bail together

# Levels of Fluffiness

Fuzzy

Fluffy

**Floofy**

**Flarfy**

# Kitten Skills 101

Voice training

Emotional regulation

Hunting

Speed

# Pip

**GENDER:** Boy

**BIRTHDAY:** June 24

**BEST FEATURE:** Soft but also pointy

**FAVORITE FOOD:** Pizza

**FAVORITE COLOR:** Green

**HOBBIES:** Annoying his big sisters

**ATTRIBUTES:** Adventurous, troublemaker

# Pip Asks: Can I Eat It?

Maybe

Perhaps

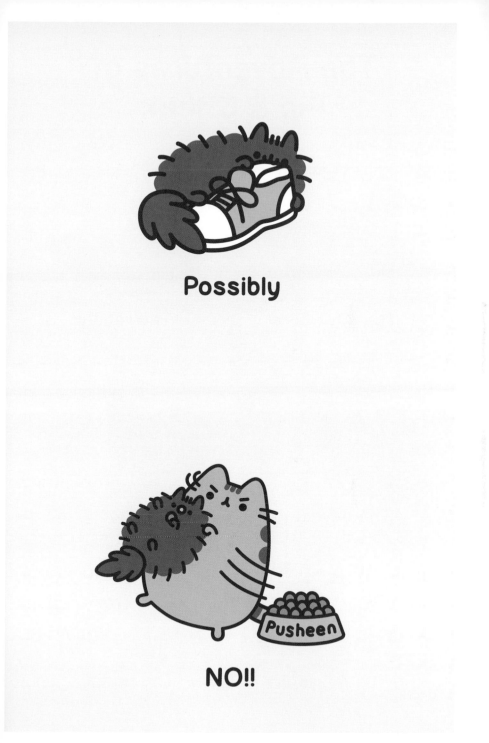

Possibly

NO!!

# The Adventures of Pip & Cheek

The adventure

The reality

The adventure

The reality

The adventure

The reality

# Pip's Favorite Things

Pip flips

Pip grips

Pip chips

Pip trips

Pip rips

kiss
Pip ~~nips~~

# Kitten Adventures
## with Pip the Kitten

The adventure

The reality

The adventure

The reality

The adventure

The reality

# Movie Night Picks

Pick a movie

Pick a blanket

## Pick a snack

## Pick a seat

# How to Tell If Your Cat Is a Superhero

## Can fly

## Has secret lair

# Fights evil

# Has an archnemesis

# Pip's Guide to Being an Artist

## 1. Learn the classics

## 2. Study from life

# 3. Explore mediums

# 4. Make OCs

# Pusheen's Guide to Having a Little Brother

## Watch him

## Adore him

Protect him

Protect yourself

# Perks of Being the Baby

**Built-in BFFs**

Meals made special

Innocent until proven guilty

# Sunflower

**GENDER:** Girl

**BIRTHDAY:** April 12

**BEST FEATURE:** Round cheeks

**FAVORITE FOOD:** Pancakes

**FAVORITE COLOR:** Yellow

**HOBBIES:** Being a great mom

**ATTRIBUTES:** Kind, always there for you

# Biscuit

**GENDER:** Boy

**BIRTHDAY:** November 10

**BEST FEATURE:** Elegant mustache

**FAVORITE FOOD:** Burgers & fries

**FAVORITE COLOR:** Purple

**HOBBIES:** Being a great dad

**ATTRIBUTES:** Kind, good sense of humor

# Pusheen Family Tree

# Only the Best for Mom

Expectation

Reality

Expectation

Reality

Expectation

Reality

# Dad Senses

## Sense of smell

## Sense of taste

# Sense of humor

# Common sense

# Things You Learn
# from Mom

## Life skills

## Good manners

# Kindness

# Patience

# Things You Learn from Dad

## How to be well-groomed

## How to dress nicely

# How to get to work

# When to take a break

# Mother's Day Gift Ideas

## Flowers

## Breakfast in bed

## A beautiful painting

## Love

# Kitty Parenting Tips

**Feed**

**Sleep**

Play

Repeat

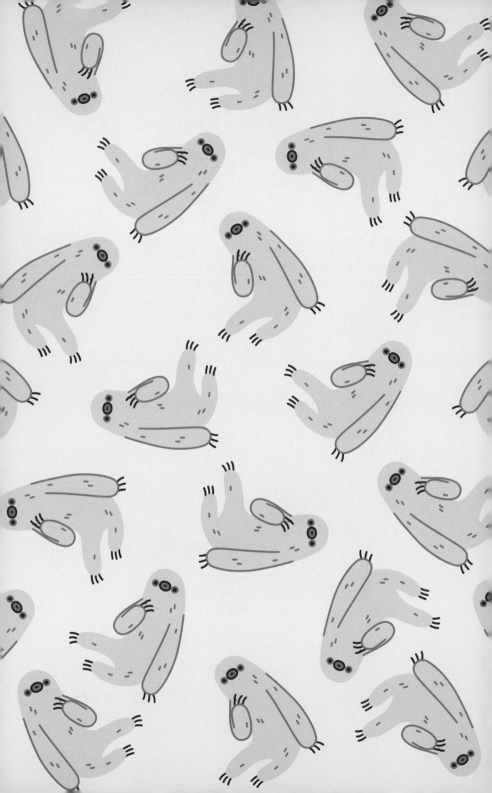

# Sloth

**GENDER:** Boy

**BIRTHDAY:** August 8

**BEST FEATURE:** Good looks

**FAVORITE FOOD:** Salads

**FAVORITE COLOR:** Green

**HOBBIES:** Gardening, yoga, being lazy

**ATTRIBUTES:** Cute, lazy, responsible

# Sloth (the sloth)

**Good at:**
**Supporting friends**

**Really good at:**
**Being patient**

**Hobbies:**
**Staring out windows**

**Best Feature:**
**Handsome face**

# Types of Friends:
# The Nurturer

**Always takes photos**

**Gifts houseplants**

**Gives the best hugs**

# Telling Time with Sloth

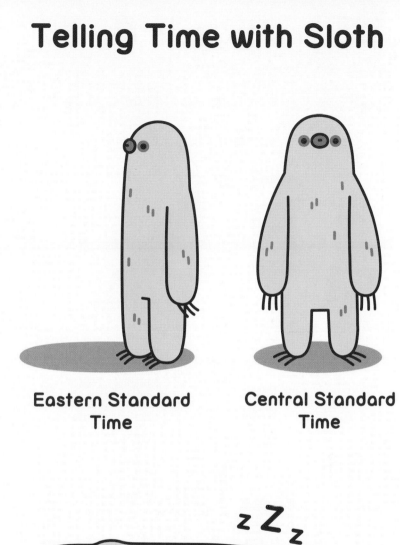

Eastern Standard
Time

Central Standard
Time

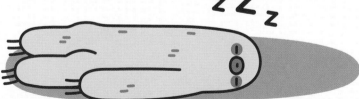

Western Resting Time

# Things to Hold On To

A branch

Spare change

## Your hat

## A good friend

# #Slothcare

## Enjoy sunshine

## Stay hydrated

# Spend time in nature

# Hug your friends

# Things Worth Doing Slowly

## Making decisions

## Sharing experiences

Creating change

Enjoying life

# Sloth's Guide to Being Devastatingly Handsome

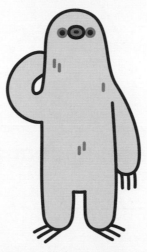

Hold yourself well

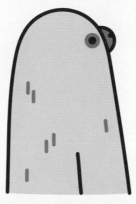

Have a nice texture

## Have some features

## Have a good heart

# Sloth's Guide to Poses

## Seedling pose

## Tree pose

## Stump pose

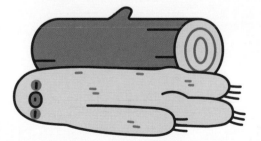

## Log pose

# Sloth's Guide to Being Lazy

## Pick things up with your feet

## Double up distractions

# Text someone in the next room

# Order takeout unnecessarily

# Bo

**GENDER:** Girl

**BIRTHDAY:** March 16

**BEST FEATURE:** Feet are also hands

**FAVORITE FOOD:** Fruits with seeds

**FAVORITE COLOR:** Blue

**HOBBIES:** Daydreaming, interior design

**ATTRIBUTES:** Big heart, big dreams

# Types of Friends:
# The Dreamer

## Loves to make plans

## Always cheers you on

## Gives advice they don't take

# Bo's Guide to
# Having a Dinner Party

Plan your menu

Decorate

Set the table

Pour the drinks

Welcome your guests

# Bo's Guide to Having a Crush

## 1. Spot 'em a mile away

## 2. Make eye contact

## 3. Confess your feelings

## 4. Undo undo undo

# Types of Parakeet Sounds

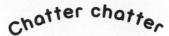

# Bo's Summer Fling

# How to Deal with Winter

Drink lots of cocoa

Get some good boots

# Check the forecast

# ~~Fly south~~ Improvise

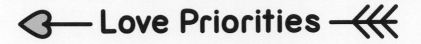

## Love yourself

## Love your hobbies

Love what inspires you

Love the ones who love you

# Bo-etry

## with Bo the Bird

**Roses are red**

**I am blue**

You're pretty

Crushcrushcru . . .

# Bo's Guide to Falling in Love

## 1. Think about them

## 2. Think about them

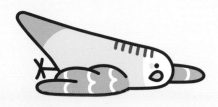

## 3. Think about them

## 4. Do nothing

# Cheek

**GENDER:** Boy

**BIRTHDAY:** May 10

**BEST FEATURE:** Mysterious rosy cheeks

**FAVORITE FOOD:** Baked goods

**FAVORITE COLOR:** Pink & blue

**HOBBIES:** Baking, playing with Pip

**ATTRIBUTES:** Tiny but hardworking

# How to Make a Cake
## with Cheek the Hamster

## 1. Mix it all

## 2. Bake it all

## 3. Frost it all

## 4. Share it all

# Types of Stars

Protostar

Red giant star

# Super giant star

# You!

# Baking for Hamsters

## Pepperoni pizza

## Chocolate chip cookie

Buttered bread

Blueberry muffin

# Things That May or May Not Be in Cheek's Cheeks

Peanuts

Cupcake

Large fries

Lost sock

Spare keys

City of Atlantis

# Types of Friends: The Foodie

Knows the best spots

Bakes for everyone

Always has room

# 4 Ways to Show You Care

## 1. Prep for them

## 2. Cook for them

## 3. Bake for them

## 4. Feed them

# Advantages to Being Tiny

**Big snacks**

**Big screens**

**Big naps**

**Big hugs**

# Daily Hamster Essentials

## Clean bedding

## A hamster ball

## A water bottle

## Snacks

# Cheek's Adventures

Expectation

Reality

Expectation

Reality

Expectation

Reality

# Pusheen's Guide to Happiness

## Practice gratitude

## Eat well

## Get plenty of sleep

# Surround yourself with the ones you love

# Acknowledgments

I would like to extend my sincere thanks to all the people who helped to bring this book to life.

Thanks first and foremost to our creative director, Katie Belton, and the whole of our creative team for all of their hard work and contributions to this book and all things Pusheen!

Thanks as always to our director of project management, Cassandra Lipin, and director of licensing, Cate D'Allessandro, whose combined organization and coordination skills are invaluable on large projects such as this book.

Thank you as well to our fantastic managing director, Mary Hennessy, for all her help running Pusheen Corp., and to my partner and Pusheen cofounder, Andrew Duff, for all that he does to support me. Their combined efforts allow me to spend more and more of my time drawing and creating!

Another huge thank-you to my ever supportive and enthusiastic book crew, literary agent Myrsini Stephanides, editors Lauren Spiegel and Rebecca Strobel, and the rest of the team at Simon & Schuster who helped to make this wonderful book!

And last but not least, thank YOU for reading it and for supporting Pusheen!

# For More Pusheen, Find Her Online